Arabesque

~

RACHEL DACUS

FUTURECYCLE PRESS

www.futurecycle.org

*Cover artwork, "Alhambra" by Karan Jain; author photo by
Jim MacKinnon; cover and interior book design by Diane Kistner;
PT Serif Caption text with Dover Heights and Hoefler titling*

Library of Congress Control Number: 2018950310

Published by FutureCycle Press
Athens, Georgia, USA

ISBN 978-1-942371-57-1

To my mother, who taught me to read, narrating in her melodious voice the meaning of letters, those arabesques on a page.

Contents

Arabesque

Caravanserai

Night Journeys

The Wishing Lamp

Golden Hat

Arabesque

Wings Clipped

Reaching too far, I may have cracked
the two bony flaps on my vertebra. The seam
shows in the x-ray, an injury
that self-soldered. My parents can't recall
when their child broke her back. The crash
evaporated into a mirror where I strained
to hold my upraised leg like a pointed wing
behind my head.

The surgeon asks if my teacher warned us
A third of young athletes and dancers
will have themselves opened,
the inner butterfly tied to the spine sheared off,
crushed and bolted together with titanium.
The bones will fuse over a slow year.
After that, the fluid joint that hinged my backbends
and arched me like a suspension bridge
will merge into a solid trunk.
I will stilt my way through the day.

All my life I wanted to be versatile
in every limb, my spinning heart
and poses bowed and curved.
My cymbaled vaults crossed
the wooden floors in long leaps.
But time aloft was always followed
by hard landings.

I was the product of an art
that let me soar into displacement.
And here I am again ready to fly.
Though the pain shoots down my hip,
I lift the ribcage, think arrow and elegance,
think gossamer.

Elegance

The changing room was painted marine blue,
with the ocean raging outside,
sea that swallowed fishing boats
slung low to the water to catch tuna.
After I changed into my pink and black
and the soft leather shoes, I entered a studio
as vaulted and dusty as the equestrian stable
I haunted on weekends. I began rigorous sets
of tendus, pliés, and battements, beating my day
into order, leg extended back—as much elegance
as I could poise, quivering, precarious,
in danger as much as those fishermen
among the slashing waves,
though it would be decades before they found
the breaks in my spine.

Arabesque penchée. Anatomy is destiny.
Perched on one leg I kissed the floor,
toe pointing to heaven, Tchaikovsky smiling
in gingerbread violins. I had yet to see myself
as in a body too short and square for grace,
see how I vogued a smile at auditions
and went onstage to family cheers.
But I grew up in a town where you scrambled
and balanced on a boat's seesaw,
all the ocean gnashing its teeth around you
while sparkling like sugarplums,

and a merciless scherzo being plucked
until the weeping notes rose in their brief solos.
I was doomed to an unrequited love
of this art, gripping the barre in a ring of sweat,
not yet knowing the grinding steps
would always keep me second from the top,
always pushing for what little elegance
I could strain into, arabesqued and strung
out on the music as if I were the violin string.

To Be Espoused

The famous poet said there are thousands
of luminous moments waiting
to be espoused by you.
I took this seriously. At the podium
he considered this very one. A small, still figure
facing a subtly shifting audience,
he meant it. I grabbed my moment
and mentally pocketed the image:
a bald man smiling inexpressibly,
impregnating the occasion with silence.

It was a moment thrilling as water
flowing into water.
After the reading, we walked to a café
and talked about these moments
that wanted us to illuminate them.
Holding our tiny espressos we felt like monks
wearing fingerless gloves in the chill of winter cells,
tracing painful curves of a gilded "h" or "g"—
what precise lines of happiness, in flecked evensong
or light on the wall. Moments seared.

We live on a bridge over the river of time,
I think he said. Or later I did. The constant sound
of history. Memory lands a few rescue boats.
We glide in them as one and hold
each other. Then we dock and go
into the unremarked bin,
entering through a central doorway.

Alphabet Scent

How do you unfurl
such luscious scent
in an alphabet?
This conversation
between my nose
and your news
is full of treats.

I always want to listen
to you, never knowing
what I'll taste.
My ears lap up
the words and continue drinking
the length of your idea,
tasting each quirk
down to your canny toes.

I'm a bear who smells
a tree's secret
hive when you talk
its savor in words that slither
honey on my furry face,
my open mouth
catching each drip.

The Honey Day

Had a honey of a day. Ate a peanut butter
and pickle sandwich, had an epiphany

while the shutters of your eyebrows flared.
It's that kind of a day. Closed my eyes

and let the fallen leaves rake themselves
into a library, each worn volume

telling a tale of spring. I woke up in the night,
before dawn, to snowflake stars.

Jolted by a quake, I stamped my foot
and stopped the planet's trembling.

I wrote you back with the eye
of a peacock feather and made
the earth laugh from beach to beach.

A View of Life from the Beach

On a stretch of powdered shells
where the surf flops and the horizon sways,
I wrestle my towel and nap, counting
each wave's smack and long-dreaming
myself more awake to each
sand grain's crystal splendor.

After a race into the sea
and a tussle with a towel,
I plan a long slide into the deep water.
Gusts of evening halfway-arc
my life's bridge. I am old but the sea

sighs softly all night in my pillow,
like the sounds of lovers
who keep reaching for each other,
and the tides of years roll me
over onto my back. I otter
on each wave's foamy tip
and again slip beneath.

Every morning, half-drowned,
I open a mango under a local palm
and read the news like a seaweed tangle,
then pop the pods
as a child does, merely for
the pleasurable whoosh
as they release salt water.

Glorious Drink

My father had captured the whole ocean
with his black-framed window.
He mined it, watching and wading
in surf, reel spinning.
Respected its power. Never turn
your back on it, he told me

after it tried to swallow me
at Playa del Rey,
the rogue wave a snake
that grabbed my ankles
buried in sand and dumped me

over, but I turned my heart
into the deep while I was in the drink,
watching seaweed drifting overhead,
light prisming in beams through the water.

I didn't want to rise from that steep dunk.
Could have drowned there
if my father hadn't fished me out.
Never turn your back
on the ocean, he yelled.

So I never did. That day I began
to drink the wine of sealight
swirling everywhere. I give myself
that pause, the betweens in life,
for a glorious daily drink,
breathing with found gills.

Fall Landscape with My Father as the Horizon Line

It looks like I'll get to pick December roses
in the week after his memorial and tossing the ashes
into his ocean. Back in Northern California,
among coral-flamed trees, our air is mild
and lightly whipped. Even in the wake of death,
beauty calls with infinity-singing leaves.
The very air is gold-tipped.
We are riffling through life's many steps
like a mad chemist clinking beakers
and holding them up to the light.
My father, inventor of rocket fuels,
was a man of explosive epiphanies.

December roses invent a new season,
a mild space for the spindled ghosts
of dandelions to float in upward dances.
I want to unfurl some new season of our relationship.
Some new horizon line, where he's steady
in a conversation about art and science,
punctuated not by predictable roses
but bolted basil, bird of paradise, cosmos,
better images for a man of surprising trajectories.

I would rather offer my father
the spade-shaped eucalyptus leaf that just fell
at my feet. Its goldenrod spine bisecting
pale celadon reminds me of one of his canvases.
He would start a painting with an ochre horizon,
then build an uncertain landscape with sand tones.
Then a swift daub with chemist's sense—dotting blue
into the gold, spreading exotic shades of green.

He captured all the greens the trees
above me are reinventing into the fire
of this new season of loss I'm entering. Clever man,
to catch hold of creativity as life's propelling drive.
Of course, a rocket man would lay hold of the force

against entropy, the life that keeps us
in motion. His way of wonder unfurls in me.
What is his new arc? I hope the unlikely roses
will spark him on and we will keep
inventing richly colored memories
of our connection, that painting
that continues to accrue its colors, layer on layer.

Monet's House Inside My Father's

Waterlilies, Claude Monet

In a house as orderly as Monet's,
the pungent colors raised doubt of seriousness.
Gingerbread moldings and geisha prints
charmed with an icy welcome
like my new French stepmother's
petit fours on a tiered plate.

I waited for dinner in my father's new home
as a guest, displaced, still in my town,
but in Monet's country, decorated, jonquil,
and never ours. Downstairs in the studio,
while I tried to converse in French,
his brushstrokes dashed across a canvas
loose as his art school hero's,
circling their impressions.

With the home of an artist of such abandon,
why did the curator whisk us
along with a neat French broom
of good taste, and why did he clear
the ashy hearthside leavings
of comfort, the way my first stepmother
removed all throw pillows from Dad's house.

Sad that the young Monets
couldn't slob around on a Saturday
in such an arranged room.
Their racket couldn't overturn
Madame's baskets of tatting,
and they couldn't be allowed
to break the Master's concentration.
A rule like the way we had to speak
French at her table.

After my father's French wife died,
the Swedish one came to stay.
Pillows could again be thrown.

His new, big paintings crowded
the white walls in their mourning grays
and rotting seaweed greens.
But I was happy to see Monet give way
to Gauguin, and the ocean to wash over
niceties like pond lilies,
and to see the green-glazed pots
go outside to be filled with perennials.
His paintings always left faces
to the imagination, so when he painted Lis,
it was with her back turned,
the cat beside on her desk.
We ate fish at Christmas and drank *glug,*
and it was never our home, but evenings,
Monet's curtains of mist came in
and eventually crossed through his mind.
I was glad that my second stepmother
had ways to curate
his house's restless, spitting tides.

Brown Suitcase

What did he have in that small suitcase
gripped in his hard right hand,
the frayed camel-colored leather and brass
clasp as adamant as the way he closed
the door on my young pleading.

What can you take away
from a thirteen-year-old daughter
on your final departure
from the windy household.
What could he have forgotten
for this last trip, from the things
that used to hang in their closet,
after he must have stolen away

shoe brush by shirt by briefcase,
his residence within our family.
For thirty years I wondered
about the alibis those items had,
but they never unpacked.
Like all his explanations,
the case remained closed.

Aurora Borealis

For Lisbeth, on her 90th birthday, 2010

She heard the green curtains of light
crackle in the stillness
as she skied home from school,
snow squeaking under her.
A girl growing up near the Arctic Circle,
my stepmother heard phone lines sing
as they froze and tightened.

The early-orphaned child
whose siblings were sent away
trekked the country alone,
humming back in a whisper
to the wires' harmonics.
She had learned never to speak much
but to do it in many languages.

Silence now invades her elder brain.
She can't always remember my father,
but she can describe skiing
under that midnight sun
and later a year living in Rome,
the daily pasta and *Ciao bella,*
when she worked as a script girl
on Fellini's crew making *La Dolce Vita.*

Smiling her wren's smile, she says
she misses her oceanside home
and my father. Their sweet life
and the roses she grew. After he died,
we moved her north to us.
She tells my brother she doesn't know
if she ate today but then tells me
about Sweden's snowflakes
forming crystalline on her eyelashes.

My Dying Brother

He's making a big house
of wood and earth, taking slow breaths
to tent his spirit in.
He's staking out a steepled risk
that life continues, holding on,
holding out for each moment
here with each heartbeat.

His big work will become a boat
to grace the waves
so he can sail into a new dimension.
The journey isn't long
and homeport is in view.
Yet his sails billow
with too much gratitude
to depart yet.

We sit on the patio outside his room.
Each awaits a turn to go in
and talk softly or help him sip.
We quietly wonder why,
with such pain, he lingers.
Slowly, without speaking, we find
that his holding onto the earth
with every hard breath is a making.

He's a good carpenter, a good gardener.
He could build a meal as beautifully
as he could sing and paint a landscape.
Now, half-asleep,
he's constructing something—
a passageway out of this room
and into the next.

He rests through the body's labor—
deceptive work that seems like destruction
but is really a building out of the elements
of dissolving an old form
into a lighter vessel to launch.

On Your Last Day You Tell Me

that life is precious. My brother,
I heard you say it in my heart as I received
word of your last breath.
Though you have given up this body
and turned away from the misery
of that hard labor to leave,
I feel you walk into the next room,
your arc now branching away.

I see how one of us always holds the other up.
One was always up and pulling along
when the other was down.
Like dolphins leaping in rhythm
we move forward and carry each other still.
As children we witnessed rooms of pain
and we hung onto our sharing that,
breathing together in refuge in a small room.

Now that your last breath has been taken
and you're free of the heavy work
of dying, I think of your splendid leap
out of that hard start. How you lofted
into recovery from addiction
and on your spread wings
lifted hundreds of others
who came to bear witness of this.

You tell me now in your deep voice
that life is precious. We must cherish these bodies
we have and hug each other
as often as we can. Precious
is the diamond in the heart,
where it is all *light*—where you are
now flying. Here we are,
and here now we will always be.

Every Morning I Try

to say a divine name perfectly,
but I can't really pronounce that swallow-swing
or enunciate the syllables a mockingbird loops.
I can't whisper the moment's name—
as it trails its white scrolls behind an airplane.

Names as pure as that
must be repeated as a flower
lets pollen fly. I should instead mimic
the closed bud's wise pause.

My human mouth can hardly shape
the million zinnias of the first letter,
let alone form the glorious close—
but I can hum the consonants
of this green-button day—
and add overtones
to the morning-setting moon.

I can echo two doves
speaking to my dog,
who rolls and rolls
on the name's final *Ah*.

Since I cannot make that purest sound,
I will get down on the grass
and roll with her, and then give
the next being I meet
a courteous consonant that dangles
the ocean in a vowel.

Arabesque

First arabesque: stand on the right leg with the left leg extended, right arm forward at eye level, parallel to right shoulder, left arm at the side, slightly behind and below the shoulder. An ornamental design of intertwined flowing lines, as in Arabic or Moorish decoration.

I.

Rising into the difficult position, hold the leg up
trembling until you can't. When you start
down the path with a dumb foot pointing
to the earth's corners in shaky tendus
and battements, being tortured en croix, endless
repetitions, hang on and sweat into the barre.

Learn that practice is dear, find art
in endlessly aiming. Arabesques earned
by each inch. The grace of swan wings
can't be fluttered into in one day
but grows subtle and articulate
as dust motes streaming through a light beam.
Bend and hold. The stretch wins opulence.

In the changing room afterward
rehearse the weight of your legs, lifting
to unroll the tights and pull on jeans.
The moment of jumping to four-four passages
echoes in your numb feet and arms
as you fall asleep, steps on the floor, a quick
pirouette into dawn. Ambition is born
in the mother lap of endurance.

2.

Precariousness. Shoulder it. Take up
the position like a cross. Ask yourself
what it's been about and come down
into that solid pillar of your own leg
under your arched body. Don't let it quiver.

Secure your inner strength like a pole
on which to hang a life's work.
You may yet have a late glide
across the stage, or you can still pose
in a moment of new-gold dawn,
a self-twirl with one hand trailing
and one pointing the way.
Do it now on a page.

3.

Live in your lovely prison,
your catenary curve
of compulsions and interrupts
of ticking longing. With family pictures
hung askew of marriages, births, deaths.
Poise yourself between them,
having stood on one leg for decades.
Your stance has grown strong.
Eyes front, slowly lift
your lichen-encrusted arms
and your fingers' wiry twigs.
Let them sprout.
Arabesque branching out.

4.

In Ugarit they baked their dictionaries,
clay tablets incised with punctures and points,
arched and tented arabesques. The idea of reading
marks may have come from the leaves'
dancing shadows. This morning the tree's
shadows script moving letters on my wall.
Likeness is our essential speech.
Shapes echo others. The eye is a leaf
and its own tear. A preying mantis
profiles a priest. Clouds coil,
and we are all walking texts
waiting to be read.

5.

Shoulder the way forward in épaulement,
accept childhood as a torso twist,
the *contr'apposto* aches of parting
and death make *la bella figura*.
Life becomes a Bernini-twist of bodies
in motion, and emotion arabesques
through pen and pain. I look over my shoulder
and pose the recursive question:
how can I seek beauty in this world
of slipped discs, gripping existence
with worn muscles and ligaments—is this
a sprain of yearning? Have I reached
too far? And yet I would do it all again,
the spiral of mistakes that led me here,
to be taut on my own bow, arrow
aiming too high, wanting too much flight.

Caravanserai

Caravanserai

*A roadside inn where travelers rest from
the day's journey, especially along the Silk Road.*

I wake to the sound of bells in the leaves,
a whispering before words, a tremble
of first light in my pilgrim bones.
Old yearnings mumble from the rafters.
This skeleton house is cramped with memories.

But the roads are young and eager.
My doorway widens as I stand here
listening to the air jingle,
as if it could buy me many things.
A siren cloud chimes in. That's it, I'm going.

I see you're on this road too.
We can walk together a few miles
and tell each other about the times
we heard the bells and rose up,
but then lay back down and hugged
a pelt of darkness.

How we let the compass grow
long in our blood, a floating needle
pointing over bridges and onto the sea's back.
How we felt its endless ache
in muscles that always knew
they were meant for dancing.

There's no logic in leaving the familiar
but no profit in clinging. Let this desert slip
into the rearview. The path is fluidly emerging.
We can stop at the inn of wanderers
and say a short hello, followed by a long jam
session of the music vibrating
on every corner of our future city.

On Foot

1.

Where I'm heading isn't on that map.
It's beyond the horizon's midsummer gaze
and the growling clouds that hazed it
dank and unpromising. Those clouds
aren't over my city. It's not Venice,
though it's also made of water.
It's not New York, but it subway-rumbas
with ancient dreams. It's not San Francisco,
though it peaks in pyramidal hope
long abandoned inside its painted ladies.
No, in my city all broken cups
and plates heal their cracks with gold.
Directions to my city briefly debate
and then fly apart laughing.

2.

My future city has lost me. I have no papers.
They flurried down a storm drain,
but then I find them quivering in a dewdrop
hanging from a leaf. My city's watery spires
and me enclosed there, a wavy angel
standing on a roof.
There's no future when I don't arrive
but no present when I leave.
My city went out the door with that man
and his leather suitcase fifty years ago.
And I'm still walking toward home.

3.

After the door slammed I grew a slum,
then a military camp, then a village
with more jewels than the Emerald City,
more populous than Bombay.
Greener than Dublin. Full of Assisi's dawn
and the Ellora caves' perfect acoustics.

The wind hums around my city's towers,
but I never mind the cacophony:
it's Beethoven played on skyscrapers:
a surf harp: a music that's beyond
rude leaf-blowing: a sound that hollows
out that slam and later intrusions.

4.

Today I set out to find
my city, but I see that no one
rides these trails except on giraffe,
and the giraffes are in another poem,
so it's a foot-sore slow-go
up to the pinnacles. There I spy
the road's heart-sinking dips
and beyond it the city's crowns.
The sky above me swallows
everything. My strategy
is to get there by backing up.
When that doesn't work, I stand all day
in an intersection and let the sun gild me.

Wine Under a Fig Tree

That any tiny winged thing
may explode from you without warning
and, after that, a long rearranging of leaves.
That you can't have too many green hands
to widen the summer evening.
That the wind's smallest breath
can rock your whole being,
root your grasp on a changeable breeze
that ever slides over and through you.

A lot to learn from a fig tree's
small white ovals. How growth
often comes in the shape of tears
yet the fat stem holds. A lot to glean
from the abundance, even after your leaves
have piled up like shoes gathered on a doorstep.
How your life's work can be picked, peeled,
and sautéed, can glisten dark and lobed
in someone else's pan. That you can give
everything and stand bare yet full of sky.
Some things a fig tree has to say
can only be said to the stars.

Things to Say to the Stars

The long-haired boy sat on the sunny wall
in front of Assisi's fifteenth century basilica
selling lavender sachets from a basket.
Cross-legged in May sunshine, twining ribbons
to close the small bags, he was the most free
person I ever saw. I offered to buy
the whole basket, to take the mountain's freshness
and pack it in my suitcase, as if to capture the way

of his unencumbered life,
though I was on a strict schedule.
The smell of the herb was pungent and his offering hand
tempted me to a new life
where I might strip off my coat
and offer it to the homeless,
like Francis of Assisi in the public square.

With things to say to the caves,
and things to say to the stars,
the young man sang in Italian, weaving
the lavender fronds and crumbling blossoms.
From his basket I caught a whiff of the generous life:
a burning and a dare, a woodsy path
straight up and out, sailing starward.

I bought as many lavender sachets
as he could pack into the largest bag
and stuffed them into my suitcase, sacrificing
a pair of Italian shoes to make them fit.
I carried them across an ocean
and tucked them into every room,
and for awhile my house spangled with peace.

Giraffes

Last night it began with a single giraffe,
and then the herd trotted through my living room
early the next morning, when the sun's honey stripes
shone through plantation shutters onto the pink wall.
Sunlight rippled over their muscular, slow-moving shoulders.
Their dark-lashed eyes glanced over shyly,
waiting to see what I'd do. The air warmed.
They wanted to see what I would do
with the dead plants on my deck,
when would I clear out the soil for fresh planting.
The giraffes were very curious.

A garden crew was blasting dead leaves
into corners, not really cleaning up,
just making a simulacrum of a well-tended garden,
blowing winter under hedges, blowing dust and twigs into heaps.
The giraffes didn't like it. They are the whales
I swam with in one phase of my dream life—
flexible, intelligent creatures so large
they could lift me out of my presumptions
onto swells and currents made by their shifting bulk.

With giraffes, it's soft air blowing you around
while they thunder by, their big breathing
a lambent pummel. Silent thunder,
they were a billowing breeze I caught
as my new life current.
On my deck I picked up every dead leaf
with cold, bare fingers—even the rose leaves
that pricked and tore my skin.
I had to handle with focused attention
every skeleton of a previous spring.

Dreams are so porous, they let real life thin
like the diaphanous muslin dresses
I wore in Berkeley those summers in the sixties,
flowers you could see through so far you'd swear

you were in a field in France. You could see through
to my dreams of being among giraffes and whales,
of whirling among things that matter
because thoughts are matter,
and around giraffes you must pay attention
if you want to survive the passing herd.

Honey Enough

for Deema

The look in her burnt honey eyes
as she cut the cake she baked
and brought to my bedside
while I was recovering—she told me
He said "Muslim" like it was a car bomb.

The way her hand shook on the knife,
unsure it was the right cake,
and words. *You understand,* she said.
I understood and deeply
considered how her black-and-white *keffiyeh*
was tied to her Middle Eastern purse
that held cake and emoluments.

Maybe it had something in there
to soothe a Jewish childhood in a Catholic town.
The scarf of otherness I could never secure
as fashionably or noose it to a handle
as she did. I told her that when I was young
the birds' *rosary* and *catechism*
flapped into my windows

and attacked. *Christ Killer,* said my friend
during hopscotch. I crossed myself
in front of the rabbi, wanted menorah and crucifix both.
Words are little explosions, she agreed.
We laughed at that, cleansed, two poets
eating a cake with honey enough
to heal any burn.

I Throw Away the Soap

After it has broken into viscous slivers
after I have lathered it into shards
after I have soaped my palms and fingers
until they slither against themselves.
After I have dug my hands into clean dirt
and soaped dust from under my fingernails.
After I have washed long enough
to sing *Row, row, row your boat* twice through.
After I have let warm water lavish
my writhing fingers
and sung the song again with the name
of my beloved.
After I have unpacked three new bars, one
smelling like summer. And put two away again.
After I have sudsed up
with almost nothing but the soap's scent.
After I have considered how long to keep
the tiny Ivory pieces.
After I have remembered how in trenches
they bartered cigarettes for tiny bits of soap.
After I have considered the piece
that was passed around a camp
as more precious than bread.
After mine has leapt to freedom
onto the shower floor.
After I have worshipped
the feeling of clean,
considered the cost of the soap
I ordered that even in its wrapper is redolent
of lemon verbena and Provence.
And only after that
With sacramental regret
I throw away the swift, slippery digit
and heft a new brick.

Sacrament

I brew the morning's coffee, tasting in its tan *crema*
a land of monsoons and a morning
when I bounced in a creaky bus
into the heart of Rajasthan, past turbaned boys
bathing in village wells and rows of banyan trees
with white-painted roots as thick as houses.
On the way to sacred tombs, half-asleep,

I once longed for a golden coffee cup,
despite the hotel's excellent chai
creamed with buffalo milk.
I was journeying through a place
I couldn't safely taste except in the hotels.
I could only smell its reality in *holi* fires
and smokes weaving through the lights
strung around a moldy pool.

Twenty years later, memory's gates open
that highway on my tongue.
In the eighteenth century, coffee sailed
from India in wooden-hulled ships,
monsoon winds infusing the beans,
changing their character from green to gold
in the way a pilgrim hopes
his journey will be carried home
in a transformation.

Now the Monsoon Malabar beans
travel to me in vacuum-zipped parcels.
I've learned that pilgrimage can simmer
in home breezes, staying in place, bathing
in the calm well of routine. I can drink
the world's sheen in photographs
and praise panoply, each sip a sacrament,
a bhajan to the sun that burnishes me,
my shoulders glowing holy.

Rain Dance with Redwood

A record waterless January
has bleached California's bones
and now we must conserve all summer
as the spoked redwoods dry and drop
skeletal fingers on sidewalks.
The poppies wither. The reservoirs
apologize to the fish. We cry,
Auntie Clouds, how have we offended?
Madre Storm, did you adopt
another country to the north?

We enter the eerie desert, deserted
by our Pineapple Express,
those long, plump weeks of rain
like whales leaping overhead.
We call to the drumming wind:
Give us your glancing hail,
your dazzling drizzle,
your soft night laments.
Come back to this stony bed.

But the wind doesn't bless us.
Water-laden clouds jealously cradle
their beneficence and swift past.
We long to skid on mossy pavements,
let dew accumulate on hair and jacket,
sip drops from the eaves,
and gulp a pure-sourced water.
We want to quench a deep
underground thirst
for what the rain embodies.

Mother Sky, give us
your liquescent blessing!
We dance for your deluge.
We sing for your billow and thunder,
and we call the season of tumbling ocean
into our hard, dry veins.

Lapsang Souchong Pine Song

*Made by slowly smoking large and thick leaves
over natural pine tree roots.*

A tea of the strongest brew. Mountain forests
in rising steam penetrate your brain's farthest point
of land and wakes you with strong shivers
on a chilled morning in camp. The sun's watery rays
pierce through pines, needling you in each sip.

Morning is being roused from your tent
by smoke, stamping into boots
and holding with wooly mittens a warm mug,
while a crazed scent invades. Pine sap.
A nearby river's revving engine and ozone
sparks flying off, plunging into your nose.

Winston Churchill drank it. Lu Tong ceremonialized
the brew in a life's poetry before dying of a nail
in the back of the head. The most extreme variety
is smoked over burning pine tar
and evokes a stogie's waft. As you brew tea, trees
and turpentine arise in the kitchen.
A forest of soaking paintbrushes grows
in your living room, all the stoic pines

and a thousand dawns of childhood
creeping into the room,
as a crispness stings your palate, then shadows:
ceremonies and conquests. Dust-mote afternoons
in the painter's studio, boredom tasting like tea
blended, instead of honey
with piney-scented turpentine.

Surviving the Dry Years

It was Biblical in California.
For seven years, the desiccated soil
erupted in a ghost dance
of skeletal weeds.
Trees grew gaunt and toppled.
A curse, of course, is how it felt.
And now an epic drenching
as an atmospheric river
big as the Mississippi
drops on us showers, gusts,
and deluges. I craft a little boat

of candles and chocolate.
I paddle upstream of big clouds.
When they part, I plan.
My sinews feel elder,
but a sense of growth flashes out
its spring lightning.
We survived: winter, drought,
glut, scarcity. Though desires grow scant,
slant, or excess, now we plant, tend,
rake the soil and smooth our skins,
secrets glowing within
the seeds' uncle,
those small but fierce hearts.

Celestial Body

The planet of his body reclines
for her fingers. Its curving roads
dip and meander to her glide
as she feels her way along
the highway he took to her bed.
She traces detours at diners
with sticky, glossy menus
and inhales the smudge of smoky years,

his beds well slept-in, many nights
following lavender twilights
and burning into lemon-sour dawns.
Beneath her touch,
waterfalls and the rivers
he sat beside listening
to his own misadventured loves,
tales of his strivings,
their crash and cacophony.

From his forehead to his shins
is a lonely treasure map.
The pads of her fingers skim
his ankles where the skin's transparent
and shows bones like boulders.
They remind her of the eons
it takes to make a world
and that our hides don't cover
as much of us as we would like.

Her touch releases yearning
in ripples and earthquakes
shearing winds in each breath,
a body's momentum,
its alphabet scent
and the slip-strike wish
to give what she is
with her travels giving.

Night Journeys

Letter from Inside a Rosebush

I've become the one *pecked at*
across the bed, air-kissed
while dashing, because it's too late
to lip-crush. Late in life and time.

I grew *invisible* just when
my pheromones started ringing gongs.
Though I can turn heads
like sunflowers following noon sun,
and I'm full of who
I always dreamed, I sing
diminuendo at home.

Yes, I may be *stubborn*
in our dilapidated castle where the mirrors
vacantly glisten. Each night I choose
escape's rope trick, my tendrils curling in
as I venture out invisible.

Pathetic. Maybe, but pathos strings
golden webs across us when we release
our messenger pigeons.
Shining networks constellate
my ringing phone.

Even though *irony* pricks my arms,
I sit triumphant inside this rosebush.
I've been here since childhood,
with the trees needing me back.
I run my loving fingers
over their cracked braille.

Reaching the Apogee on an August Midnight

During a stretch of bad years,
I took my walks at two in the morning,
treading miles of worry as I passed
dark yards. One August night,
my feet propelled me toward the moon
that flared up pale and webbed
from behind the hill.

I swung along as scenes of love
and guilt lit up the dim windows.
I watched people's lives in houses,
how they swift away too fast
as the moon sails down the abyss.

The wind guilted me
with honeysuckle and sage.
The dross floated out of me.
Aromas opened as I plowed
a dark sea, feet pounding.

My losses clicked.
To live hurt like music
but motion was remedy.
A pinpoint beam
on the mountain's flank
picked out a zigzag road.

I spangled with the moon,
each of us hanging in a void.
A thorn, the moon has never left my side.

Friday Night Fable

I rest on a bench after my night walk.
Old bone, soft rifts, blood bleached,
I breaststroke the July dark
while Venus hangs
close as a porch light.

Windows across from the lot flicker
with red lanterns and Motown.
They rock behind the curtains
while the music revs like the Mustangs
zooming late down the street.

I hide in the corners of my eyes,
wanting to dance in the shadow
of this cricket-loud oak. Unable
to go home to my own life
and its diminishments, I'm switched on
in this fable of Friday night.

I watch the moon rise and flex
his round biceps and I bite
into that apricot flesh,
but when I hear footsteps
and a young face rounds
the corner, I flee. Shameless,
that false star, daring to wink at me.

Transparency

My superhero showed up dead drunk
on dilithium crystals,
which he had brushed against
while trying to fix the ship's warp drive.
A likely story, I said, knowing
he had conflated myths, and seeing
the way his red and blue colored suit
had bled together to make him purple man.
He staggered to the couch and sprawled.
I got him a glass of water,
but he asked for something
with color and more strength.

It's not so often a man like that
asks you to come to his rescue, let alone
at 11:49 at night, or slurs
that crisp Midwestern speech—
to say nothing of his perfect
but now flattened hair revealing
two cowlicks and a balding patch
at the back of his well-shaped head.

I was not only civil, I was gallant,
or as gallant as a girl should be
to the man of steel when he's a molten mess
and weighing down one end of her couch,
muttering random slanders to the lamp.
Then he pleaded—so sad
to see him beg. I told him to swing
up his feet onto the other end—he thought
I would join him, but I just wanted
the couch to be balanced
under his weight. I knew as soon
as he was horizontal, he'd be snoring.

Later, when my hero woke, full
of apologies and vague come-ons,
he was sober. So much less

interesting. He pleaded ignorance
of dilithium and the effects
of galaxies far, far away, but of course
I saw right through him. His excuses
for not-so-noble behavior
had been foiled by the effects of drink,
but even before that I could tell
because my x-ray vision turned him
transparent as air. The only trouble now
is all heroes have an inner tarnish.
Though some girls might think
that's actually a good gift,
faster than a speeding bullet
at sussing out love's land mines.

Recycling

I fed the pages of our estrangement
into a shredder's steel teeth.
I let go proof, belief, and faith.
I sliced into ribbons
the alphabet of evidence.

I let go dependence
and tore into bits the duo
photographs. The paper fell away
in curls, in arabesques
of calligraphy. Crinkled hurts
spiraled into the bin.

Even without paper, we wrote
furiously for years of blame.
We scrolled even on the sliced strands
and filed the wounds into folders,
suspended them and then scribbled on
more dark regrets, to be thumbed
soft again and again.

But if we want to go on,
we can't let the detritus
spill across our washed carpets.
We must make mulch
of the pulp, learn new scripts,
clean the shadows of our erasures,
and virgin our leaves
with ruthless forgetting.

Among Strays

Sometimes the cats stray to you
on your night walk. Ginger
and white cats, fleeting passage
with small mews, a stealthy rub
on your ankle, and the way they roll over
at last, as if they knew you
as they know the stars.

Sometimes their eyes take shape
in the chair nearby.
They're curled invisible
in full feline wisdom
and summoned to care for you
despite the gray morning's bleakness.

The feral cats want to be known
and felt. Their company
bests your abyss. They make night wandering
a shapely shift of veils
as they wisp across the moon's
bright tarnish, helping you understand
your own straying. Their eyes shine
into yours. A rumble of silver clouds.
You shelter in the shadow of the other.

The Round Dance Floor

Tonight the stars outdid the crickets
and teamed up with me
to salsa bump waltz
on the sky's round dance floor.
We clung, those stars and I,
bone-deep and tendon taut,
hips grinding together,

strung-out and pulling
the earth under us
yard by yard, gathering it
into a rug of loam, honeysuckle
sizzling as we pressed our cheeks together.

The stars and I
were strangers touching hands
for a photo shoot, the intimacy
of unknowns.

Even when we separate
and I go inside, we will carry
each other's pulses like an earworm
concert, heaven and earth
rolling their pillows closer together.

Launching from Old Roots

After Beth Moon's photograph "Aquila,"
from the series "Diamond Nights"

Sometimes diamonds,
sometimes old roots,
sometimes it's a bent arrow
that shoots out of your head,
pointing toward Arcturus,

as if you could catapult
yourself and thrust out
of first stage, then second, and up
into the stratosphere
as if from a starry launchpad—

as if you might begin
the journey infinity poses
as a riddle, into a connect-the-dots
web of numberless connections,
into a night reincarnated
from all the old wishes
tossed up into time
by your shaggy head—

as if you could loose
all your leaves like tiny rockets
and rise with your bare crown
as the new being vaulting
into a diamond-filled, black lake.

Repairing with the Filament of Red Spiders

I stepped out on the deck this morning
to clouds leaping overhead like whales
breaching the blue and small red
spiders suspended between the plants.
I swept them into corners with my broom
and reset

       their daily task
as mine, watching the whales
retreat from me, your gradual absence
knifing through our webs,
giving me a daily task of repair
from a single point:
to leap

       an ocean of loss
I can't float in all night,
so I keep stroking
the unconquerable,
leap by leap.

       Like a whale
or spider carrying the thread
forward in the dark, in secret,
the fine filaments of spiders who,
while we sleep, breaststroke

       through the void.

When I Got Up

the roses were waiting for breakfast
and Italy was still made by hand.
I sat on a stone sill
and smelled the twining lavender
and rosemary. Smiled back
at the carved gods
on the fountain.

When I got up it was November
in Assisi but August here.
The grapevines baked
at eight a.m. A rabid dream
condensed and hung on the lily's lip,
only to be scooped up
by a hummingbird's tongue
that reached past it into the sky.

I let go and flowered.
The day was fresh,
but so were my wounds.
Horns hooted. The road beamed.
A flare of sunlight insisted I open
my heart to you again.
I got up, and did.

Lighting the Lamps

Even the lamps are brighter
since we turned back to each other one night
in a small room at the cusp
of the Valley of the Moon,
where the Miwok built cone houses
of twigs and ate acorns and elk.

Here we are again, lighting the lamps
of sense, in this place
where a forest and a mountain unite.
When morning sun stripes the walls
and we're far from home, it glints
brightly and comes undone
in rainbows from the mirror's bevel.

You turn from looking to me,
and the flick of your gaze
rekindles those mornings
when we could feel the sky
opening its gracious cape
of clouds sailing, white and slow,
above the ark of our room.

The Next Morning Journey

One touch from you and I'm awake,
standing at gratitude's threshold.
All I've done is lose, but perhaps that's why
I'm showered by a fountain
of dawn, my senses
wild in the light's fluidity

and longing only to give
someone hungry a rare fruit.
The wish streams down
on my head. I raise wings
I didn't know to use
and catch a breeze to soar up

and rescue for you this:
these first rays and a flight
of rattling hummingbirds
who feud through the trees—
those dervishes aloft
in prayer-like whirling.

The Wishing Lamp

Foundling

Mother, you found me fresh
and fondled my small face, ears, and toes.
A foundling yourself, you opened
your blanket to let me into a soft space
where I grew, sometimes sheltered from the rage
of winds that rapped hard on the windows
of our house and then blew you off course.

I tucked in and hid from the down-suck.
Father as an ocean gale to whip.
When your wrecked ship's tug
pulled me down, I vaulted
from the hard-walled crib.
Through a slip of pronoun,
a change of person, I found
the trick of becoming.

Found the grammar of standing
in your place and the verb
slack to ride the undertow
and drift to sea, where tides
no longer rip but parallel the land.
I floated this way into middle age,
swimming with long strokes,

and again found myself
on a white beach where you, ashore,
elder and smiling in your yellow cap,
hold open a dry towel.
Shivering, I climb in and let myself
be finally found safe.

The Buried Part

Why did I think of an underground river
with its secret torrent heart
at the sound of the word *Mother*?
The chilly ions' breeze and a moving maw. *Ma.*
It's the buried part of her that inspires dread.
Her surface a calm fog. What she called her lack
of mother instinct. The undercurrent that pulled
so I couldn't write to the birth mother,
I want to be your baby's mother.

That river still thunders into crevices
and boulders my script. How can I admit
I don't want my life smothered
under the weight of another,
the way she wilted under shouldering
the tonnage of a woman's life.
How can I ask her now
about the picture of me, three days old
in her limp arms, find out what ice
was forming under the pall on her wrung face?
If I do not ask, it will soon be too late.
But my question lies buried.

Stealing Eggs

Fluff, dust, and burbling, then pecks, beaks, and squawks in the coop, dense with feathers. The soft creatures startle and ferociously nip. The man in the small henhouse, a soft-voiced stranger, was a grandfather I had met once before, his glasses square and reflecting my gaze. When we picked him up at the Pentagon, they saluted. My mother was afraid to let me go to gather eggs. Nervous as a hen, she held my hand for a moment and then let go. He slipped a hand into mine and gently pulled. Inside the coop, he slid his palm under a chicken without even ruffling her as he drew out a warm, blue egg. He put it in my hand. I thought of fried eggs. I didn't know it could have grown to be a chicken. Then the quiet man with poor eyesight took my hand and we stole quietly away, back to the house and my glad mother. I never saw him again.

Freckled Fritzi

She sat up while fast asleep and whooped like an Indian, my Russian aunt told them over pancakes in camp. She had come from the East to share my pup tent, call me *Dollink,* and tease me about my constellations of freckles. She herself was a spangled sky of flecks. No one in our family knew when Fritzi was making things up, but her tale shone on me the spotlight of their surprise. She was short, as if mallet-squashed. She smoked cigars and dyed her hair Lucille Ball red. Descended from a family of cabinetmakers who fled the pogroms for a land of Fords, Fritzi became a psychiatric social worker. She loved to scandalize the relatives, who said, *Fritzi, what next?* And she grinned, the gap between her teeth like the gulf between family factions. Getting up at sunrise, in the wood smoke and pine chill, I sat on a campstool wearing a blanket, listening to a din of birdsong. She told the tale again of my war whoop, and my parents and brother laughed while I lit up Fritzi Red. Later, she took me to the tide pools and showed me how to tickle open anemones. When our green eyes met, I lit my torch from her blaze.

New Year's, San Felipe

Fishing rod propped in a spike, my father drank tequila and sang Louis Armstrong songs on New Year's Eve, capering in the surf. His reel squealed as the line raced through, unnoticed. Giggling, he fell asleep on the sand.

In the morning we walked down the beach, peering into tide pools. He reached down, scooped up a dark blob, and handed me a tiny, squirming octopus. The water baby slithered in my hand—velvet-wet softness in this hard expanse. A gift fished out of murky depths and released to float in the years between us.

Rooftop Flying

We shinnied up the white trellis, climbing over a skimpy bougain-villea, scratched by long thorns. Intent on reaching a height above the family storms. My brother was dragging a tablecloth up, tucked into his shirt. He stood on the graveled roof and pulled it around his shoulders as a cape, standing super, sending gravel flying down onto the driveway, intentions clear. I'd like to fly away from the thunder in our father's voice, away from a man who made explo-sions for a living, the bipolar rocket engineer who developed the world's most explosive missile fuel. The man whose voice preceded him into a room and into the whole neighborhood, a bark that could send us into decaying low earth orbit before the crash. Our father did not believe a man should go to the moon, though "To the moon, Alice!" was his favorite quote. My brother had been launched this afternoon, after helping Dad clean fishing tackle. We scurried up, our rivalry turned all solidarity, the neighborhood roofs gleaming and empty. We were alone in the sky. That wide moment we shared before coming down.

The Pancakes

We had them everywhere we traveled. Browned around their edges and butter-dripped, Mom fried them in a silver pan at home, on the Coleman stove in camp. Pancakes on the beach, in the mountains, in redwood groves, where the sizzle was so loud even the birds couldn't drown it out. Yeasty, with a texture like the sandy soil I once ate, just to see. The maple syrup was always real and warm as her quick hug, if you wandered by while she was waiting for the bubbles in the cakes to pop so she could turn them over. There were always more than enough. How did she do that, when everything else in our family was so few and slim, cool to the touch, the air with a stale ocean taste, and on some days a tuna scent from the canneries. But our pancakes always smelled rich and wheaty, thickly piled on your plate in concentric rings, as if to make up for the rest of our lack. They were most delicious right after the front door slammed behind Dad, its hollow wood reverberating like his last blast. Those pancakes never deflated, never sank in on themselves as my mother's face did when he left that last time. And even then there were pancakes for that first breakfast when the house went solo of him. Nothing ever since has tasted so sunlight-skimmed.

Everything Is Relative

to my mother's keening sobs
at the sink guilting me,
and the sound bank-shots off
the rising of my husband's voice,
and then her voice on the phone decades later
when I'm still innocent of her grief,
until a bird at the feeder tips out
a Mozartian shrill of queenly accusation.

It's my husband's keyboard slouch,
the sack of rotted vegetables in the fridge,
a bin of recyclables no one will take out.
Guilt smolders in the relativity of our relatives.
Like the rockets my father launched
from Cape Canaveral, explosions
that defined him as does my lifelong flinch
at banged doors, dropped cups,
and sudden, alarming shouts,
it scathes the silent atmosphere.

Einstein's definition of the universe
was taffy-fluid. So I put on running shoes.
Everything is my relatives.
Relative to the observer's velocity.
Maybe if I sprint faster, more space
will dilate time and distance me
from them, let me lope ahead of myself
and break the tape—except that time's

again bending, and I bump into my father,
once a panther, now a prune in a dish.
His mother whimpering at light speed
from her years-long deathbed.
His father, who rockets
from a creaking chair. Though I run faster,
as Einstein predicted, the more I escape,
the more they close in.

The pull of time and space to my origins
is a black hole now. I travel inside
its sucking well until, memoiring,
I pull near the heart of it. The one
heart we share, the thread running through
family—love and its thwarting—unless
we attain the speed of forgetfulness.

Wishing Star

That last summer we sat
in creaking saddles on day trips
in the High Sierra, inhaling petrichor
and lichened bedrock.
We nudged cattle through tall grass.

I had all I ever wanted at thirteen:
my own horse and a long August.
Above the cabin, stars buzzing
like mosquitoes. I knew the seasons
to come wouldn't have horses
and as many stars.

This morning above my suburban town
trees gallop in the wind, flexing thin branches,
green and gold leaves whipping around
themselves like a horse
that bucks when backing up.

I have hooked my star
to dawn's grapefruit moon.
Boughs creak like saddles.
My wishing star, gone on a long ride,
vanished in the August meteor shower.

The news said a chance of more
meteor showers later.
That made me buck and back up.
I heard the call of lost mountains.
At sixty-five, I spin around,
and prance downhill

to the valley of lost things,
in a sweet lope to where a new trail
starts and the underground river
cuts deeper, flashing dark lights.

Bird Bones

I'm making a book, putting in the bones,
and then feathering it with words.
I saw the way to bind it
yesterday as I sat with my friend
at her picture window,
looking out on a field
at her bird feeders.

As we talked, I watched a goldfinch
feed on the perch.
Then he swooped straight into
the window and died, breathtakingly.
We looked down.

There was no question
he was nearly dead, wings spread out
on the ground. So fast, from feeder
to death. Bird bones are hollow, you know,
as light as life.

My book will contain his arched wings
spread on the soil like a striped cloak
and his pale yellow beak, which opened once
and closed as he died, clearly calling *Ba-ba!*
piping through the bones of memory.

The Camel's Teeth

Just when the suns slides offstage
and rounds the eaves, I need more light—
so I seek a lighthouse's revolving flash
as it skewers the mist, and I carry home
flickers in a pack on my sloping shoulders.

I always want what's slipping away,
what's beyond the obstacles.
Because, in autumn's procession
of animals, the camel leads.
His desert-cropping teeth never stop.
A roof rat pebbles into my dreams.
A small brown snake of rain
swishes between my toes.
The camel's teeth pulp us.

Every night in winter I contemplate
the ceiling's fine print, how it annotates
what I have left. Lap blankets, socks,
pillows, fingers, almost all toes. I count
among the ambient imps this dwindled light
and re-angle the blinds to succor the sun
when it breaks open again. I clutch at sparks

and then descend sleep's internal cave.
I become a blind deep-sea fish
who navigates with bioluminescence.
I listen to the stems rotting.
It's dark when I wake, but then shuttered light
stripes the wall. Though I am crunched
between those hard teeth, I rise
and touch the glass and snow beyond
from the warmth of this side.

The First Wish

She's moving smoothly under me,
so I pick up the pace, guiding my horse
with a shake of reins to change direction,
leather over her neck with a light slap
as we trot down the eucalyptus alley
between streets in Palos Verdes.

The most alone a teenage girl can be
is on a horse she was told not to gallop
but still nudges faster beneath dangling fronds,
down the wide park-like median
toward the curving cliffs of Redondo Beach.
I have my wish, first of the body.

A short girl holding taut a large animal
learns her way. I counter the pull
with gripped thighs to restrain her lope
until we reach the stinging whisk of salt air.
This is nowhere near as difficult as ballet,
but like my first day at the barre,

I stop short of straining ligaments
and find how to not be perfect yet.
Pulling up to the hitching post,
I dismount. We expel huge breaths,
grandly spent, drinking in
the whole ocean's ringing grandeur.

The Second Wish

Turritopsis nutricula, *the immortal jellyfish, is a hydrozoan whose medusa, or jellyfish, form can revert to the polyp stage after becoming sexually mature.... Theoretically, this process renders the jellyfish biologically immortal.* —Wikipedia

Almost the first wish the genie hears
every time it pops out
is *immortality.* And rare's the one
who can tell what the genie looks like:
an empty mirror or a bottle full of water.

A few have said he looks like a jellyfish,
one of zillions who live backward
like Merlin, slowly becoming
their own babies who again start to age,
eternal life their cage and drudge.

Touching others they share the curse—
but only when asked. Immortality.
What could be worse?
I'd find another jellyfish and wish
for love, not life, to be immortal.

Golden Hat

Cool Shoulder

In autumn, when the earth turns a cool shoulder
to the sun and the sky gets that faraway look

like a woman trying to decide how to decline
an invitation, I want to feel my singleness

on this earth, unique and lone
as when desire's bones fit too tight to my flesh.

I crave the loneliness to spite it, the kind
that makes my feet hungry for new miles.

Passing a field of feathered grasses,
I want to be brushed senseless,

then to slip between sky-piercing pines,
and there I want to pine—but for whom?

The trodden weeds are not more lowly
or gold-beaten than I, declining in fall.

At this season, with a sky so blue,
I want to bite its shoulder.

The head-size stones in a rock wall
turn, each, a different face.

Each rock pretends
it doesn't know me. A woman

is raking piles of leaves into neat humps.
I want to shake her hand and kick them open.

Golden Hat

The hour is turning and the tide's
repeating verse breaks open.
I have drunk its bitter spume,

Today will be shorter than yesterday
by a moon's edge. All things revolve
while I summer a little longer.

And here is the sun sinking at the last.
He always makes me laugh in his golden hat.

A Lighter Way

Drifting down lightly,
the tiny charcoal and white
bit of fluff stopped me,
breathless, as it swung

down a ladder of air,
back and forth,
a feather with swaying hips.

I thought I knew how changes
come, in inch-long
increments, in lurches
that interrupt the stately dance—

but the feather stopped midair,
me the weight of births,
marriages, and deaths,

the dropping down
of each event, if I let them
all pass, nearly in flight.

Birthday Peonies

The flowers arrived
without fanfare, handed to me
at the door by messenger, with a card
I had to hunt for, then could hardly read.
A surprise of rosy explosions.
Unpacking the dozen flowers
from a paper cone, each sheaf
of petals emerged as a whirling planet.

I laid them on the counter
to prepare for water
by smashing the woody stems.
Their fragrant fireworks
crept through the kitchen
like the simmer of floral soup
or the aroma of nearly baked cake.

I placed each flower at an angle,
crossing them to anchor
in the widemouthed vase.
Each seemed composed
of tiered butterflies.
I set the vase on the glass table,
which reflected twelve round heads.
Each flower was a wing
stretching wide, being
remembered, a flutter in my pulse.

Rules of Faith

You have to apologize to the trees
when you're discovered in glee.
You're no longer allowed to speak
the consonants of dawn's crystal,
only to disparage despair as it pedals past
on its rickety bicycle.

The pact is silence, beauty muted
except to speak in five-lobed oak leaves
or in the trees' octopus limbs.
You may describe the finches
fiddling Paganini but not say a word
that voices the pinwheels on the dark,
the traveling galaxies.

You can't say *I am that*
when stellar light blossoms
in your brain or umbels like a jellyfish
through the ocean of your blood.
You may not speak of wings
in your breath when you take in
too much autumn. You must apologize
for odes birthed quick as quintuplets.
They shock the nursery.

Cone of Silence

I drove away from the zone of household debate seeking undisturbed space, expecting nothing but the dust of the local bike path. Though it was Sunday, the chainsaws were going and cars shooting into the lot like comets. I put on walking shoes and entered the din. But suddenly I became a cone of silence, moving and drinking in airy syllables of leaves. As a listening swath I swept between trees, creek, and houses, stretching up. The saws brayed and the engines shushed but now behind a curtain of quiet. A skater rolled by with a smart nod. I passed the yard of fancy chickens. Turning deeper into the woods, I melted into the cups of gold poppies and the pattered lisp of firs. My senses dipped deeper into the waters of sound and gathered them around me like a luxurious ball gown, the folds' smoothing swish absorbing inner noise now. Silence deepened and broadened, its origins in everything I passed. A yellow finch sang silence from a branch. A pine twisted it in its wind-weaving arms. Houses four-squared it on a hill. I found it possible to be a funnel of benign abyss, a taking in of each singular beat.

The Penthouse

What can I write? No matter how much
my body grips pain, or my heart does,
I live inside a jewel of vast geometry.

From an old chair in a field I look up
at clouds drifting in layers of self-opposition
and see my crowding thoughts
as people rushing, knowing they're too late.

Petals float like birds, birds
like petals. I open the door

of my losses to the glint of the gem's facets.
My chest opens. The lens focuses
on a choreography of a thousand thousand
leaves. The past falls away
like a sparrow across the sky.

I live in the penthouse of paradise.

The Music Room

The room I live in tunes up
even before I open my eyes.
Through the closed window come beeps,
squeaks, and trills growing louder,
joined by the thrum of wheels
as they bump on the freeway's cement seams.

The heater's whoosh enters my pulse
as if I were cupping my hand to my ear
to magnify every least motion of air.
Even the sizzle of my tendons straining
against the covers and a spatter of rain
dotting the panes become the notation
of my day's random concert.

I attend the music like a conductor,
choosing my world, from a first peek
at the oak's pale green leaves
twisting out of grooved branches. I choose
the silver flutes of house finches and muster
my skill to maestro skidding tires
and whistles into a harmony
my air-braiding finger leads.

Next I elect the office melodies,
adding a chickadee's tumbled notes
to the jackhammers' timpani
as it rumbles through the window glass.
I grab that sound and wave in
the computer's buzzes, signal the woodwind
hum from a conference room,
and let the day croon to me.

Only when all the instruments
have played do I rest
my baton and let silence come
singing its utter solo.

A Presence So Near

Every rumpled green hill
leads straight up to a blue sky
that shrugs loose a herd of clouds.
They graze away behind the mountain.
The oak trees grow luminous shoots
on coiled black limbs.

I'm caught in a pause.
Every grass blade's silver
shivers me awake.
Something divine is so near
that my steps slow
so as not to miss
its stately cascade.

How had I missed the gold
in the air all week? When I ran
by the tall tips of cherry trees,
I was busy shattering silence.
Words hid the bird that agreed
with a fountain
and all its sunlight choirs.

My prayers are reduced to the leaves
that sieve the air like lovers
endlessly repeating each other's names.
I go inside and find an orchid
altar enough. Its tapering petals
curve, my white sails
ready to embark.

The Third Wish

Amid the exploding rockets
in the newspaper's every line,
one morning I see a new world.
I see it out my window
in an icy November
as I stand looking down at a parking lot
where trucks back up and turn
with great dusty clatter, then leave.

Their beeps and grinding roar
into my bedroom, and yet a stillness
hovers in the pale shapes of people
loading the trucks with food,
their shadows softened in the light
of a dawn-descending moon.

And I then see, as if dreaming,
a boat rocking on the sea,
riding toward an entirely new earth
that unfolds inside this old shore.

More trucks come and unload vegetables
and fruits rescued by volunteers
from a grocery's waste.
The noise builds. There's no question
I'll go back to sleep. People shout
as they lift crates full of greens
to ferry to the dank pavements
where some of our neighbors
still live in this old,
want-filled world.

As these shadows work, rays
from the east soften the concrete
as if this newest world is dawning
in golden white. Simple care
upwells. One by one, we take up

our places as the ancient moon sails
down the blue-black sky.
This old room where I live
dwindles. My shoulders round
in praise, and I turn away to dress
and find my place.

The Map of Light

One bird outside my window repeats *Sweet,*
Sweet, Sweet. Another answers *Rock, Rock.*
I guess I'll go to a place called Sweetrock.
I googled. It seems to be a farm in Portland
where they grow herbs, bake artisanal bread,
and make Swiss pastry. How my day proceeds:

by poetry and association, as when I was five
and asked my mother how my oatmeal
is named by birdsong. A chain
of associations dangles my every day.
When I learn that my breakfast comes
from the town where I went to school
on the top floor of a firehouse,
the surprise makes me bounce.

Signs call out to me, their beaks
full of verbs and nouns, pulls and tugs.
I'm familiar now with the subtle snap
of a tether that pulls me through the woods,
between ancient mossed limbs soaring
like obelisks because they too are pulled—

and, yes, this is how I navigate.
My day is strung on a web of words
appearing on box flaps and phone poles.
I shouldn't confess that I feel them ringing
in my bones, or that spider-silk
connections riffle me like a stream,

watery ribbons of inkling that lead me
out of the woods and past stop signs.
Or that I let myself hopscotch hunches
and skim the soil. Or that I like walking
this way, lifting from a logical stride
to shimmer into the sky's map of light.

Grains of Monet

Grainstacks, Claude Monet, 1891

He loved grains
    of wheat and snow, particles
massed in brushstrokes
    of insight that say the vast and opulent
        universe is full of echoes, each leaf
    mimicking its neighbors and
my eye seeing them, all parallels and panoplies,
        snowflakes, whitecaps, cloud flurries.

The sherbet glee painted into stalks and steeples,
      a tree's singularity beheld
    with a fly's complex eye,
sweeping the eons, putting every sun
        in the Horsehead Nebula into the bristled
haystack. A sun-crisped field dancing
    with a billion limbs and lingams,
      a grass blade's shaft
    dividing each integer of being
      to an eternal prime.

The River

Cookies crumble in the pockets of my jeans.
I save them in case I need extra good fortune.
The one today told me to relax, and I remember
my mother always said, *What are you waiting for?*
But then she also said, *Why are you so impatient?*
She couldn't have been right both times.
I just grabbed the nearest cookie,
and as I chew and swallow the pieces,
they melt into the same thing: loss, anger, joy,
swirling down the stream beyond
the restaurant. I left it winking
at the statue of Lao-Tzu on his ox.

Take some more, they said,
I took a hunk of architecture,
some random windows—open, close.
I took the cheapest ticket, the desperate caress,
the stolen insight. Moments flowed
through my ears, whispering
that nothing is ever lost, just changed
into memory. I should have done more
with my life. I should do less and relax.

All time exists at once.
I think Einstein said that, or Lao-Tzu, breathing
down my neck, wanting his river back.
I cross carefully, my shoulders
wearing wings of fog.
I step on small islands, all the gone souls
I have ever known blooming and scented
as they hang around my neck.

Blessings

Yesterday my bedridden stepmother
uncharacteristically said God
was blessing us, blessing her,
and that blessings shower all around us.
What makes this shrunken woman
with a broken pelvis lying in bed
feel blessed? All her ninety-five years
are behind her. She can hardly remember
who she is, and yet she sees a light

streaming on her in this nursing hospital's
off-gray walls, despite the falling away
of her body. I wonder how she came
to be one of those who sense angels.
I wonder how she knows she is blessed
and through what telescope she sees
beyond her broken flesh.

People often seem to feel blessings
around someone who is dying.
And after, a celebration. We were all so jubilant
after my brother's funeral.
We had such a raucous party.
We toasted him, played his music,
gloried in stories of his life.
And now, nearing her last,
my stepmom feels this parade nearing.
She hears its trumpets and cymbals.

Is she sitting up in her light body
and then walking out to join
the procession of herself—
as if her life was a great work
and completing is a hallelujah moment.
Friends will gather with us, flush in memories,
all saying at the end, after the hug,
we've been blessed. It's the dark
season now, and so good
to think of light. To know a new solstice
awaits. And we turn, as into an open door.

Acknowledgments

My gratitude to the editors of literary journals and anthologies where these poems first appeared. I thank them for their dedication to poetry, which helps sustain mine.

A Narrow Fellow: "The Honey Day," "When I Got Up"
Atlanta Review: "Rain Dance with Redwood"
Avatar Review: "Caravanserai," "Golden Hat," "The Music Room"
Blue Heron Review: "The Penthouse," "Cone of Silence"
Comstock Review: "So Near" (Muriel Craft Bailey 2016 Contest, Poem of Special Merit)
Eclectica: "Wishing Star," "Brown Suitcase," "A Glorious Drink"
Gargoyle: "A View of Life from the Beach"
Gingerbread House: "Transparency"
Mockingheart Review: "Giraffes"
One: "Elegance"
Panoplyzine: "Wings Clipped," "The Third Wish"
Peacock Journal: "Sacrament," "Cool Shoulder," "Launching from Old Roots," "Reaching the Apogee on an August Midnight," "To Be Espoused," "Blessings," "Everything Is Relative"
Pirene's Fountain: "The Camel's Teeth," "Friday Night Fable," "Repairing with the Filament of Red Spiders," "Honey Enough," "The Round Dance Floor," "Lapsang Souchong Pine Song" (*Silk Road* anthology)
Postcard Poems: "The Second Wish"
Prairie Schooner: "Bird Bones"
Prick of the Spindle: "Wine Under a Fig Tree"
Prime Number Magazine: "I Throw Away the Soap"
The Cortland Review: "Every Morning I Try"
Valparaiso Poetry Review: "Grains of Monet"

About FutureCycle Press

FutureCycle Press is dedicated to publishing lasting English-language poetry books, chapbooks, and anthologies in both print-on-demand and Kindle ebook formats. Founded in 2007 by long-time independent editor/publishers and partners Diane Kistner and Robert S. King, the press incorporated as a nonprofit in 2012. A number of our editors are distinguished poets and writers in their own right, and we have been actively involved in the small press movement going back to the early seventies.

The FutureCycle Poetry Book Prize and honorarium is awarded annually for the best full-length volume of poetry we publish in a calendar year. Introduced in 2013, our Good Works projects are anthologies devoted to issues of universal significance, with all proceeds donated to a related worthy cause. Our Selected Poems series highlights contemporary poets with a substantial body of work to their credit; with this series we strive to resurrect work that has had limited distribution and is now out of print.

We are dedicated to giving all of the authors we publish the care their work deserves, making our catalog of titles the most diverse and distinguished it can be, and paying forward any earnings to fund more great books.

We've learned a few things about independent publishing over the years. We've also evolved a unique, resilient publishing model that allows us to focus mainly on vetting and preserving for posterity poetry collections of exceptional quality without becoming overwhelmed with bookkeeping and mailing, fundraising activities, or taxing editorial and production "bubbles." To learn more about what we are doing, come see us at www.futurecycle.org.

The FutureCycle Poetry Book Prize

All full-length volumes of poetry published by FutureCycle Press in a given calendar year are considered for the annual FutureCycle Poetry Book Prize. This allows us to consider each submission on its own merits, outside of the context of a contest. Too, the judges see the finished book, which will have benefitted from the beautiful book design and strong editorial gloss we are famous for.

The book ranked the best in judging is announced as the prize-winner in the subsequent year. There is no fixed monetary award; instead, the winning poet receives an honorarium of 20% of the total net royalties from all poetry books and chapbooks the press sold online in the year the winning book was published. The winner is also accorded the honor of being on the panel of judges for the next year's competition; all judges receive copies of all contending books to keep for their personal library.

www.ingramcontent.com/pod-product-compliance
Lightning Source LLC
Chambersburg PA
CBHW070001100426
42741CB00012B/3100